GUESS HOW MUCH I LOVE YOU

To Liz with love,
A.J.

First published 1994 by
Walker Books Ltd
87 Vauxhall Walk
London SE11 5HJ

This edition published 2005

10 9 8 7 6 5 4 3

Text © 1994 Sam McBratney
Illustrations © 1994 Anita Jeram

The right of Sam McBratney and Anita Jeram to be identified as author
and illustrator respectively of this work has been asserted by them in
accordance with the Copyright, Designs and Patents Act 1988

This book has been typeset in Cochin

Printed in China

British Library Cataloguing in Publication Data:
a catalogue record for this book is available from the British Library

ISBN 1-84428-108-6

www.walkerbooks.co.uk

GUESS
HOW MUCH
I LOVE YOU

Written by
Sam McBratney

Illustrated by
Anita Jeram

WALKER BOOKS
AND SUBSIDIARIES
LONDON · BOSTON · SYDNEY · AUCKLAND

L ittle Nutbrown Hare,
who was going to bed, held
on tight to Big Nutbrown Hare's
very long ears.

He wanted to be sure that Big
Nutbrown Hare was listening.
"Guess how much
I love you," he said.

"Oh, I don't think I could guess that,"
said Big Nutbrown Hare.

"This much," said Little
   Nutbrown Hare, stretching out
his arms as wide as they could go.

Big Nutbrown Hare had even
longer arms. "But I love YOU
this much," he said.

Hmm, that is a lot, thought
Little Nutbrown Hare.

"I love you
as high as
I can reach,"
said Little
Nutbrown
Hare.

"I love you as high as *I* can reach," said Big Nutbrown Hare.

That is quite
high, thought
Little Nutbrown
Hare. I wish
I had arms
like that.

Then Little
Nutbrown Hare
had a good idea.
He tumbled
upside down
and reached
up the tree
trunk with
his feet.

"I love you
all the way up
to my toes!"
he said.

"And *I* love you
all the way up
to your toes," said
Big Nutbrown Hare,
swinging him up
over his head.

"I love you
   as high as
I can HOP!"
   laughed Little
      Nutbrown Hare,

bouncing up
   and down.

"But I love you as high as
I can hop," smiled Big
Nutbrown Hare – and he
hopped so high that his ears
touched the branches above.

That's good hopping, thought Little Nutbrown Hare. I wish I could hop like that.

"I love you all the way down the
lane as far as the river," cried
Little Nutbrown Hare.

"I love you across the river
and over the hills," said
Big Nutbrown Hare.

That's very far, thought
Little Nutbrown Hare.
He was almost too sleepy
to think any more.

Then he looked beyond the
thorn bushes, out into the big
dark night. Nothing could
be further than the sky.

"I love you right up to
the MOON," he said,
and closed his eyes.

"Oh, that's far," said
Big Nutbrown Hare.
"That is very,
very far."

Big Nutbrown Hare settled
Little Nutbrown Hare
into his bed of leaves.

He leaned over
and kissed him
good night.

Then he lay down close by
and whispered with a smile,
"I love you right up to the moon –

AND BACK."